Dad Jokes

The Good, Bad and Just Plain Silly

Copyright 2020 by Hayden Fox All rights reserved.

This document is geared towards providing exact and reliable information in regards to the topic and issue covered. The publication is sold with the idea that the publisher is not required to render an accounting, officially permitted, or otherwise, qualified services. If advice is necessary, legal or professional, a practiced individual in the profession should be ordered.

- From a Declaration of Principles which was accepted and approved equally by a Committee of the American Bar Association and a Committee of Publishers and Associations.

In no way is it legal to reproduce, duplicate, or transmit any part of this document by either electronic means or in printed format. Recording of this publication is strictly prohibited and any storage of this document is not allowed unless with written permission from the publisher. All rights reserved.

The information provided herein is stated to be truthful and consistent, in that any liability, in terms of inattention or otherwise, by any usage or abuse of any policies, processes, or directions contained within is the solitary and utter responsibility of the recipient reader. Under no circumstances will any legal responsibility or blame be held against the publisher for any reparation, damages, or monetary loss due to the information herein, either directly or indirectly.

Respective authors and companies own all copyrights not held by the publisher.

The information herein is offered for informational purposes solely and is universal as so. The presentation of the information is without a contract or any type of guarantee assurance.

The trademarks that are used are without any consent, and the publication of the trademark is without permission or backing by the trademark owner. All trademarks and brands within this book are for clarifying purposes only and are owned by the owners themselves, not affiliated with this document.

Where are dad jokes saved?

In a dad-a base!

How did the pirates stay fit?

They did planks!

What is a belt made of watches called?

A waist of time!

How does a Kleenex dance?

With a little boogie in it!

Is that a pile of kittens over there?

No, it's a meow-tain!

Where did the robots meet up?

The circuits!

Why did everyone at the party get a cold?

It was sick!

Who's the girl that sounds like an ambulance?

Ni-na, Ni-na, Ni-na!

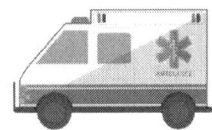

Why was the boy scared of the speed bump?

He couldn't get over it!

How do you get a squirrel's attention?

Act like a nut!

Why was he fired from the rubber band factory?

He snapped!

When is your dentist appointment?

At tooth hurt-y!

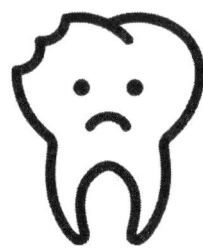

Where did the baby cat go swimming?

In the kitty pool!

What's a vegetarian zombie's favourite food?

Grrrains!

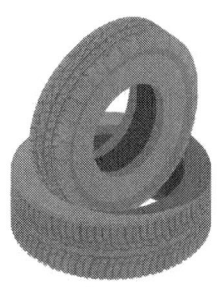

Why couldn't the bicycle move?

It was two tired!

Why was the sponge so arrogant?

It was self-absorbed!

What did the evil chicken lay?

Deviled eggs!

Why was the strawberry late to work?

It was stuck in a jam!

What is a cow with no legs called?

Ground beef!

What happened when the girl hit her sister?

A cry-sis!

What did the mouse say after eating the cheese?

It tastes Gouda!

How does the Easter bunny stay healthy?

He egg-cercises!

What did one tree say to the other in spring?

What a re-leaf!

What do computers snack on?

Microchips!

What did the drummer name his daughters?

Anna 1, Anna 2!

What happens when you mix an elephant with a fish?

Swimming trunks!

Does that clock have any hands?

No, it's an all-arm clock!

What did the carpet say to the worrisome floor?

Don't worry, I got you covered!

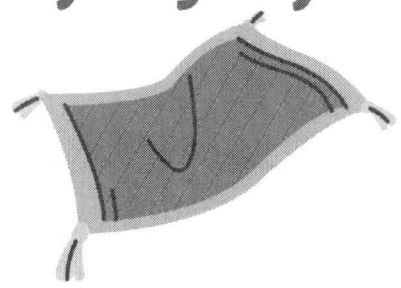

How did summer come to an end?

Autumn-atically!

What plant can only be found in the past?

A nost-algae!

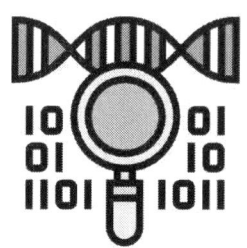

How do you differ girl genes from boy genes?

Their genetic makeup!

For what reason did the coach visit the bank?

To get his quarter-back!

Why did the past, present, and future go to the bar?

They were tense!

What secret did one eye tell the other?

Between us, it smells!

Why couldn't number 4 jump into the pool?

He was two squared!

Why did the man sell his pizza machine?

He kneaded the dough!

What do you call chasing a train?

Running track!

How do mermaids clean their fins?

With Tide!

Why did the snowman scour the bag of carrots?

He was picking his nose!

Why was the boy scared of Santa?

He had Claus-trophobia!

How come the broom arrived late?

It over-swept!

Is it true that Canada is a real country?

Seems like it's all maple leaf!

Why did the acid have an attitude?

It was a-mean-o-acid!

How did the headphones call their friends over?

They said, "Come ear, buds!"

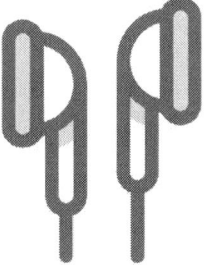

Is it safe to dive into the pool?

It deep-ends!

What breed of dogs do scientists love?

Lab-radors!

Why were 1 and 3 jealous of 2?

Because it was Tuesday!

Hey son, did you take a shower?

Why? Is one missing?

What did the glove say before leaving the ball?

Catch you later!

Why doesn't he trust taking the stairs?

Because they're always up to something!

Did you trip when you were in France?

Eiffel over!

What's a house's favorite clothing?

Address!

Why is that bird wearing a wig?

Because it's a bald eagle!

Who's the magician that lost his magic?

Ian!

What's a rich person's favourite tea?

Property!

Why was the computer hungover?

It took too many screen-shots!

Do you like the new blender?

I've had mixed results!

What do athletes have before a race?

Nothing, they just fast!

Why is the graveyard gated?

People are dying to get in!

What kind of bears don't have teeth?

Gummy bears!

What do cows enjoy reading?

Cattle-logs!

Why was 16 sick after dinner?

Because he eight and eight!

What did the mummy play at the dance?

Wrap music!

How do you woo a baker?

Bring flours!

What does the Queen enjoy in the afternoon?

Royal-tea!

Why can you not eat a clock?

It's too time-consuming!

Why was the picture sentenced to jail?

It was framed!

What made the tomato red?

It saw the salad dressing!

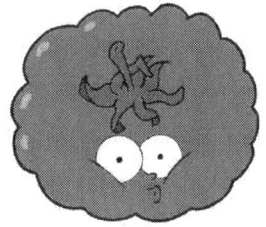

Why did the cell phone want glasses?

It lost its contacts!

What's a fish without an eye called?

Fsh!

Why did the tailor go on vacation?

Because he seemed stressed!

Any chance you need an ark?

Because I might Noah guy!

Do you want to hear a construction joke?

Actually, I'm still working on it!

Did you read that anti-gravity book?

I couldn't put it down!

Which dinosaur is the smartest one?

The thesaurus!

Why do mountains make good comedians?

Because they're hill areas!

Why did the dad joke cost $1000?

It was a grand-dad joke!

What's purple and smells just like blue paint?

Purple paint!

What makes money and freshens your breath?

Invest-mints!

What did the buffalo say before leaving his son?

Bison!

What happened when the hula dancer went boxing?

Hawaiian Punch!

Where did the frog's car go?

I think it got toad!

Why did the bridge need a pen and paper?

Because it was a drawbridge!

What animal is the worst driver?

Pigs, they always hog the road!

Why was Sir Galahad always so tired?

He worked the knight shift!

What's Dracula's favorite holiday after Halloween?

Fangs-giving!

What kind of ball makes the most noise?

A racquetball!

How come the teddy bear refused dessert?

Oh, he's already stuffed!

What does BMW stand for?

Big Money Waste!

Why don't crabs have many friends?

Because they're shellfish!

What did the accountant name his son?

Bill!

What do wolves eat for breakfast?

Pigs in a blanket!

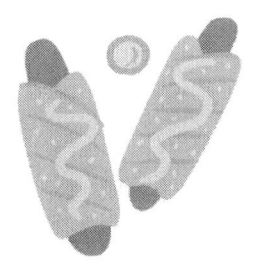

Why don't vampires make good teachers?

Too many blood tests!

What sound does a witch make when driving?

Broom, Broom!

Have you been to the gun range?

It might be worth a shot!

What happens if you step on a grape?

It lets out a lil wine!

Why did the chef fire the boy from the restaurant?

He was all up in his grill!

Why was the alligator wearing a vest?

Because he was an investigator!

What happens when an ice cube gets upset?

It has a meltdown!

What do you call an unattractive dinosaur?

An eye-saur!

Why shouldn't you trust atoms?

They make up everything!

How did the water become holy?

I boiled the hell out of it!

Why was the mushroom so popular?

Because he was a fun-guy!

What begins and ends with disappointment?

Your report card!

Where do gorillas go for drinks?

The monkey bars!

Why was the fish wearing a tie?

Because he was so-fish-ticated!

What do you call a cold sandwich?

A brr-ger!

What happens when a dinosaur has a crash?

Tyrannosaurus wrecks!

Where did the crayons go for a holiday?

Color-ado!

Why didn't the rabbit like the comb?

Because it teased hares!

Why did the skeleton miss the party?

It had no-body to go with!

Why did he give away the vacuum cleaner?

It was just collecting dust!

What candy is never punctual?

Choco-late!

Why did the driver cover his eyes?

The light was changing!

What do you call a belt made of cardboard?

A waist of paper!

How did the shoemaker end up in heaven?

She had a good sole!

What vitamin do sharks need?

Vitamin sea!

How does a snowman travel?

By icicle!

Why didn't the fish get in trouble?

It was off the hook!

What do fingers tend to grow on?

Palm trees!

What do you call a boys' math club?

The Algebros!

How do snakes get into a house?

They Slytherin!

Knock Knock
Who's there?
Beehive
Beehive who?
Beehive nicely and open the door!

Knock Knock
Who's there?
Alex
Alex who?
Alex the questions around here!

Knock Knock
Who's there?
Jess
Jess who?
Jess me and my shadow!

Knock Knock
Who's there?
Beets
Beets who?
Beets me!

Knock Knock
Who's there?
Dishes
Dishes who?
Dishes your friend, open the door!

Knock Knock
Who's there?
Heaven
Heaven who?
Heaven you heard enough of these jokes yet!

Thank you for reading! If you enjoyed the book, leave us a review and let us know what you liked or what you would like to see next.

As a special bonus, enjoy this exclusive preview of one our other popular titles!

250 Would You Rather Questions

A Clean, Fun and Hilarious Activity Book for Kids, Teens and Adults

How To Play

Step 1

Split into two teams whether that be boys vs girls, kids vs parents, or any other mix of your choice. If possible, also assign one person as a referee.

Step 2

Decide who gets to go first. Which team can do the most pushups? Which team can guess the number between 1 and 10 from someone not playing the game? Or just a good old-fashioned rock paper scissors?

Step 3

The starting team must ask a question from the book and the opposing team has 10 seconds to not only choose an option but to also give a meaningful reason as to why they chose what they did. The referee decides whether the answer is acceptable.

Step 4

The team can discuss their answer together but only one player can give the answer. The person answering must alternate every turn.

Step 5

If the player who is answering can't choose or give a good reason, then that player is out for the game and can't answer anymore or be involved in the team discussion.

Step 6

Repeat until all players are eliminated.

Questions

1. Would you rather live one life that lasts **1000** years or **10** lives that last **100** years each?

2. Would you rather use eye drops made of vinegar or toilet paper made of sandpaper?

3. Would you rather be 4'0 or 8'0?

4. Would you rather be super strong or super fast?

5. Would you rather take a guaranteed $120,000 or take a 50/50 chance at $1,000,000?

6. Would you rather be in constant pain or have a constant itch?

7. Would you rather go forward or backward in time?

8. Would you rather never be able to take a hot shower again or eat hot food again?

9. Would you rather never play or play but always lose?

10. Would you rather be a vegetarian or only be able to eat meat?

11. Would you rather be a chronic farter or chronic burper?

12. Would you rather be deaf or mute?

13. Would you rather have a third eye or third arm?

14. Would you rather age from the neck up only or neck down only?

15. Would you rather be only able to shout or whisper?

16. Would you rather never touch an electronic device again or a human?

17. Would you rather have a mediocre short term memory or bad long term memory?

If you enjoyed this title, check out our other books by searching "Hayden Fox" on Amazon!

Printed in Great Britain
by Amazon